◇ SPRING ◇ ACTIVITIES

SEASONAL PROJECTS FOR KIDS

Written by Denise Bieniek
Illustrated by Dana Regan

Troll Associates

Metric Conversion Chart

1 inch	= 2.54 cm	1 pound	= 0.45 kg
1 foot	= .305 m	1 cup	= .24 l
1 yard	= .914 m	1 pint	= .473 l
1 mile	= 1.61 km	1 teaspoon	= 4.93 ml
1 fluid ounce	= 29.573 ml	1 tablespoon	= 14.78 ml
1 dry ounce	= 28.35 g		

Conversion from Fahrenheit to Celsius: subtract 32 and then multiply the remainder by $\frac{5}{9}$.

Contents

INTRODUCTION

Dear Teacher,

Spring is here, and with it comes an end to fitting bulky coats in closets and cubbies, an end to running out of tissues for all those runny noses, and best of all, an end to being stuck indoors all day. I eagerly anticipate spring each year because there are always so many things to do with the children. And after cleaning out and rearranging my closets, I often find old lesson plans and scraps of paper with ideas written on them that are perfect for a gorgeous spring day.

Spring inspires me to help my students grow and change. I promise myself that I will put together all those paper scraps into comprehensive and organized seasonal files, that I will find new and interesting places to see and visit for field trips, and that I will finally clean out that cabinet under the sink that I have been putting off for the entire year. And your class is sure to feel just as inspired as you welcome the new season together.

In writing **Spring Activities**, I have found many new activities that I have enjoyed sharing with my class and other classes in our school. I have included our long-time favorite projects, and some new ones as well. Of course, the children's best-loved activities tend to be those that are messier in nature—but they wouldn't be children if that weren't so.

We had a lot of fun with these ideas and we hope you will too. Happy Spring!

Denise Bieniek, M.Ed.

Name _____

March Goes in Like a Lion and Out Like a Lamb

How many things can you find in this picture that begin with the letter L? Circle them.

Can you think of any other words that begin with the letter L? Write the words on the lines provided.

_____   _____

_____   _____

_____   _____

_____   _____

The Festival of Dolls

In Japan, the Festival of Dolls, a traditional girls' holiday, is celebrated on March 3. Young girls take out their collections of dolls, many of which have been handed down to them from generations of ancestors, and display them proudly for all to see. The dolls are usually delicate and have very intricate detailing.

Ask students to bring in dolls from home so that they may have a classroom Doll Festival. Display the dolls and encourage the children to give some background information about their dolls, such as where they were made, how old the dolls are, special clothing, and names they or previous owners may have given their dolls. Then help students make new dolls for their collections by following the directions below.

Materials:

- ◆ oaktag
- ◆ scissors
- ◆ plain and patterned fabric scraps (muslin, cotton)
- ◆ craft glue
- ◆ fiberfill stuffing
- ◆ buttons
- ◆ yarn
- ◆ permanent markers

Directions:

1. Make patterns for a doll head (circle), body (rectangle), and arms and legs (smaller rectangles with rounded edges) from oaktag.
2. Trace each pattern onto fabric scraps twice. Place one half of each set on a flat surface with the printed side face down.
3. Squeeze a line of glue around the edges of each body part, leaving an opening at the bottom. Place the matching body part face up on top, as shown.
4. Gently stuff the body parts with the fiberfill stuffing and glue the openings closed, as shown.
5. When all the parts have been stuffed, glue them to the body at the appropriate places.
6. Use buttons to make facial features and yarn to make hair. Provide students with markers to add any additional features.
7. Use the remaining patterned fabric scraps to make clothing for the dolls. Trace the doll's body, arms, and legs onto fabric, then expand the lines about 1" outward. Cut two pieces of fabric and glue or sew the pieces together (leaving openings for feet, hands, and neck) to make shirts, pants, and dresses, as shown.

Classroom Communications

Tell students that Alexander Graham Bell was born on March 3, 1847 and had one of his most important inventions, the talking machine, patented on March 7, 1876. Bell found a way to make sound travel through wire to another room, where his assistant was working.

Explain to the children that before the telephone, people communicated in other ways. Ask students if they can think of some ways people without telephones could communicate (i.e., word of mouth, drums, body language, horse, pony express, series of noises, and writing or drawing).

HELLO?

HELLO?

Divide the class into small groups and tell them they will be creating ways to communicate ideas other than speaking and writing. Give the following sentence as a conversation starter: "I am hungry." Then allow the groups about five to ten minutes to come up with a way to show the meaning of the sentence. Encourage the groups to share their work by acting out their ideas. Then progress to more difficult ideas, such as "Let's go swimming," "I love you," or "Let's have a party."

Display books showing the types of ways people communicated from primitive to modern times. Distribute crayons, markers, and paper so that students may draw their favorite form of communication. Ask each child to include what type of communication it is and why he or she likes it. Hang the children's work on a classroom wall, or bind the pages into a book and display in the school's library.

My Own Telephone and Address Book

Materials:
- ◆ crayons or markers
- ◆ scissors
- ◆ loose-leaf paper
- ◆ stapler

Directions:

1. Reproduce the telephone pattern on page 11 once for each child. Ask students to color the pattern and cut it out.

2. Help each child write down his or her family name and address on the lines. This will be the cover of the telephone and address book.

3. Have children cut pieces of loose-leaf paper to the same size as the cover.

4. Gather the pages together, with the cover on top. Staple the pages along the left side, as shown.

5. Have students take their books home to fill in with their families. The children may wish to write in the names, addresses, and telephone numbers of their friends or family members. Encourage children to write down emergency numbers as well.

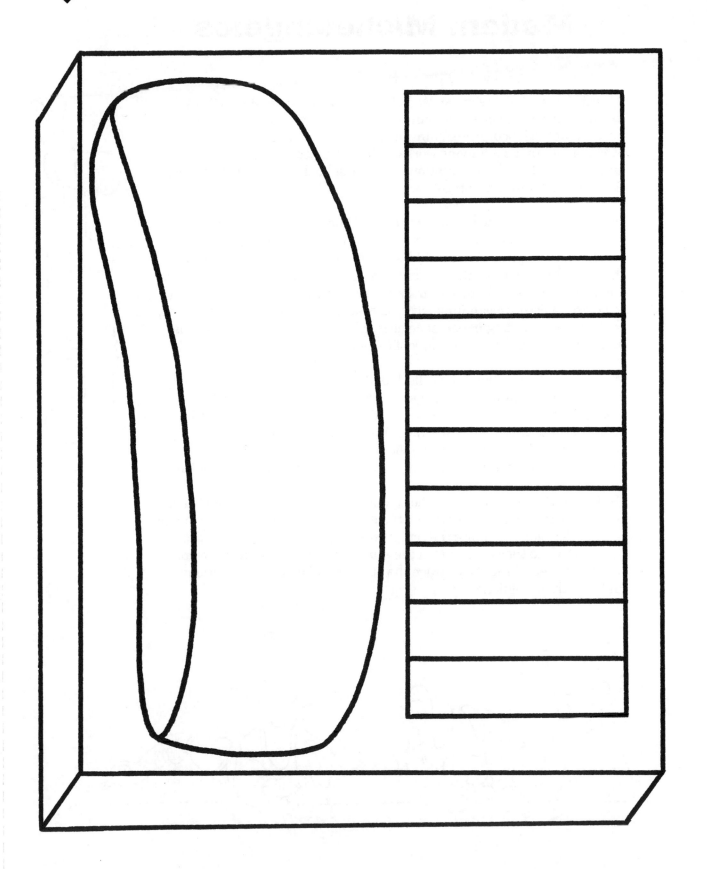

Modern Michelangelos

Tell the class that the artist Michelangelo was born on March 6, 1475 in Italy. He was involved in many different things, all of which revolved around the arts: sculpture, painting, pottery, and architecture. Michelangelo's most famous works include sculptures called the Pieta and the David, and The Creation, a painting he did on the ceiling of the Sistine Chapel in the Vatican.

Display books or show pictures of some of Michelangelo's sculptures, as well as sculptures by other famous artists. Discuss materials that might be good for sculpting (i.e., marble, some woods, metal, clay) and some that might be too difficult (i.e., fabric, Styrofoam, banana peels). Tell the children that they will be making sculptures of their own. Ask students to begin collecting clean junk, such as boxes, empty plastic bottles, cans, containers, wrapping paper, shoelaces, ribbons, wiring, string, jar lids, and anything else they can think of (no glass).

When enough junk has been collected, divide the class into small groups and lay a pile of junk in front of each group. Encourage students to discuss and vote on what they would like their group's sculpture to be, either representational or abstract. Within those categories they may wish to twist their ideas to make them humorous or exaggerated. Provide students with masking tape to use to assemble their sculptures.

Gather all the groups around the sculptures for a class discussion. Tell the artists to talk about what their sculptures represent, how they came to their decisions to create the sculptures, any interesting things that occurred while they constructed the sculptures, and their own interpretations of their work. Encourage the other students to ask questions and give their opinions.

Harriet Tubman Day

SLAVERY

FREEDOM

UNFAIR

GOOD

MEAN

FAIR

WRONG

KIND

In recognition of Harriet Tubman Day on March 10, gather the class into a circle to discuss the topic of slavery. Begin by writing the word "slavery" on the chalkboard. Then ask students to name whatever comes to mind when they hear this word. Write their comments around the word "slavery" on the chalkboard. Remind the class that there are no wrong or right answers; they may say whatever they are thinking.

After everyone has contributed, talk about the comments by putting them into categories on a large piece of oaktag. Ask students to create the categories and identify the comments that should be listed under each heading. If possible, let students read *Nettie's Trip South*, written by Ann Turner (published by Macmillan). This story, about a girl from the North who visits the South and is appalled by the idea and conditions of slavery, is a good book to use to expand the discussion about slavery.

Then ask the children to consider the topic of slavery from the slave owners' point of view. The slave owners believed slavery was a great system since they could obtain free labor. All they had to do was provide the slaves with the barest of essentials: food and housing. Point out that many slave owners did not care that this situation took tremendous advantage of other people. Some slave owners, however, reconsidered their position of slavery during their lives and set their slaves free before being forced to do so by the government.

Ask students what they would have done if they were the son or daughter of a plantation owner who had just inherited the plantation and all its slaves. Provide the children with background information about Harriet Tubman. Tell students that she was a former slave who helped over three hundred slaves find their way to freedom on the Underground Railroad, which was a series of "safe" houses where slaves could rest and be cared for while on their way North. Many remember her for her courage and determination.

The Night I Met Harriet Tubman

1. Ask students to think for a few minutes about what it must have been like to be an escaped slave. Remind the class of the conditions under which most slaves lived and how slaves felt: they were uneducated in the ways of America; poor, hated, distrusted; made to feel inferior; separated from family and friends; sad and lonely. Encourage students to describe how they might feel if they escaped, knowing there were men and dogs out tracking them down, and the horrible punishment they were sure to receive if they were found.

2. Then ask the class how they would feel if they were directed to Harriet Tubman and experienced her bravery and inspiration.

3. After discussing their feelings, distribute paper and have students write down or dictate a story entitled "The Night I Met Harriet Tubman." The children may wish to include their feelings about slavery, the conditions under which they lived, their escapes, their hopes and expectations, meeting Harriet, and the outcomes of their escapes.

4. Encourage children to share their stories with the class. Display their work on a classroom wall or a bulletin board, or bind into a class book and place in the reading center for all to see.

Johnny Appleseed Day

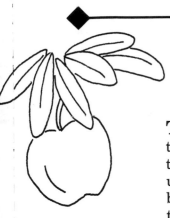

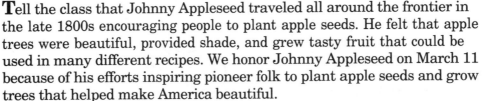
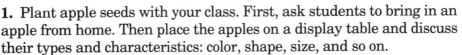

Tell the class that Johnny Appleseed traveled all around the frontier in the late 1800s encouraging people to plant apple seeds. He felt that apple trees were beautiful, provided shade, and grew tasty fruit that could be used in many different recipes. We honor Johnny Appleseed on March 11 because of his efforts inspiring pioneer folk to plant apple seeds and grow trees that helped make America beautiful.

1. Plant apple seeds with your class. First, ask students to bring in an apple from home. Then place the apples on a display table and discuss their types and characteristics: color, shape, size, and so on.

2. Have an apple tasting party. Slice the apples in quarters and let students sample each type. Discuss and identify the tastes: sweet, sour, bland, and so on.

3. Save the seeds from each type of apple. Categorize them according to apple type and discuss any obvious characteristics.

4. Let the children try to grow their own apple trees. Place about 4" of soil in small plastic cups. Mix in some pebbles and gravel to help the water spread. Using one finger, make a shallow indent in the soil about 1" deep and place a few seeds inside. Then cover the seeds with soil.

5. Water the seeds every other day. Be sure the plants have plenty of light. Measure the growth with a craft stick by inserting a stick into the soil next to the cup's side and down to the bottom. As the seeds grow, draw a line indicating the height of the seedling every other day.

6. Compare and contrast the rates of growth of each tree. Each child may graph the growth on a bar graph, as shown. Have students list the dates along the bottom from left to right. Then tell students to write the heights along the left side from bottom to top. Draw a seedling from the base line to reach the height indicated on the left side.

	4/2	4/6	4/9	4/10	4/12	4/14	4/16
1 1/2"							
1 1/4"							
1"							
3/4"							
1/2"							
1/4"							

MY SEEDS' GROWTH BY JENNY

Solar System Mobile

Materials:

- Styrofoam balls of various sizes
- paints and paintbrushes
- paper cups
- scissors
- construction paper
- black thread
- long sewing needles
- clothes hangers

Directions:

1. Help students research books for information about the planets in our solar system, which is called the Milky Way. Identify the names of each planet: Mercury, Venus, Earth, Mars, Jupiter, Saturn, Uranus (discovered on March 13, 1781), Neptune, and Pluto.

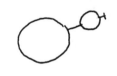

2. Point out the relative size of the planets to each other and their colors. Lay out Styrofoam balls on each work area table along with cups of paint and paintbrushes. Then ask students to re-create the planets, as well as the sun, using the Styrofoam balls and paint. Allow children opportunities to look in books for guidance in selecting the colors and sizes for the planets.

3. After the paint has dried, children may wish to cut out rings or moons for their planets from construction paper.

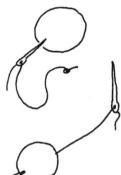

4. To hang the planets from the mobile, thread a needle with black thread and knot the ends. Insert the needle through each planet. When the knot touches the planet, cut the thread at the needle and remove it.

5. Tie the planets to the base or top section of a hanger. Attach the sun first at one end of the hanger. Then add the planets in order of distance from the sun, as shown. When the hanger is swung gently around in a circle, the planets should revolve around the sun.

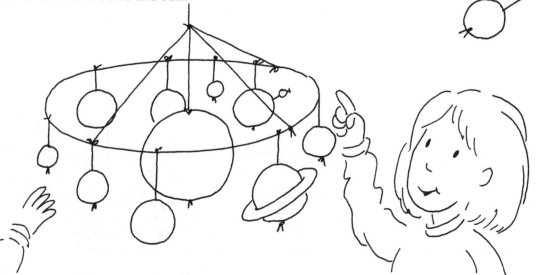

Outer Space Bulletin Board

Materials:

- ◆ black bulletin-board paper
- ◆ small containers, cardboard rolls, construction paper, foil, tissue paper
- ◆ scissors
- ◆ crayons or markers
- ◆ glue
- ◆ collage materials
- ◆ stapler or tape

Directions:

1. Cover a bulletin board with black paper. Tell students that they will be creating an outer space display. Ask them to brainstorm on what they should include on the bulletin board.

2. Lay out small containers, cardboard rolls, construction paper, foil, tissue paper, scissors, crayons or markers, glue and collage materials. Encourage the children to design planets (both real and imagined), rockets, and space creatures.

3. Attach the space articles to the board.

4. Children may wish to add stories or short descriptions of their outer space board, such as names and characteristics of planets and creatures, the sounds one might hear, outer space travel, and adventures one might have while in outer space.

Four-Leaf Clover Place Value Activity

Materials:
- ◆ crayons or markers
- ◆ scissors
- ◆ tape or magnets

Directions:
1. Reproduce the clover pattern on page 19 ten times and cut them out.
2. Write a number from 0 to 9 on each clover, then color them.
3. Attach the numbered clovers to the chalkboard with tape or magnets. Then call out a two-digit number and pick a student to come to the board. Ask that student to choose the clovers showing those numbers, and place them in the proper place value order. After students become adept at this activity, you can increase the challenge be calling out three- or four-digit numbers.
4. To vary the activity, place numbers together on the board and call out a number that uses all the numbers shown, but in a different place-value order. Choose a volunteer to unscramble the number.

Limerick Time

Explain to the class that limericks are five-line, funny rhymes that typically use the a-a-b-b-a rhyme scheme. Teach students the following limerick, then have the children make up limericks of their own.

> *There once was a girl named Lynn,*
> *Who was so incredibly thin.*
> *In the tub she had lain,*
> *Then she unplugged the drain.*
> *And promptly got sucked right in.*

To make a St. Patrick's Day bulletin board, reproduce the leprechaun patterns on pages 22-23 several times. Assemble the leprechauns and color the figures. Then display the children's limericks around the bulletin board, as shown, with the leprechauns as seasonal decorations.

Movable Leprechaun Puppet

Materials:

- ◆ crayons or markers
- ◆ glue
- ◆ oaktag
- ◆ scissors
- ◆ hole puncher
- ◆ brass fasteners

Directions:

1. Reproduce the leprechaun patterns on pages 22-23 once for each child. Help students color the leprechaun patterns.

2. Help each child mount the patterns on oaktag and cut them out.

3. Punch holes where indicated on the patterns. Then show students how to use brass fasteners to attach the arms, legs, and head to the body.

Leprechaun Action Poem

Teach the class the following poem about leprechauns. Students may use their movable leprechaun puppets to dramatize the poem.

Did you see what I just saw?   *(place hand over eyes)*
Over there, behind the door!   *(hide leprechaun behind back)*
Up on a chair! Down on the floor!   *(move leprechaun up then down)*
I've never seen a leprechaun before. *(shrug shoulders while shaking head)*

If you catch one, some folks say,   *(wrap arms around leprechaun)*
Make three wishes right away.
One, two, three!   *(children do three tricks with leprechaun)*

Spring Planting Experiments

Materials:
- ◆ plastic cups
- ◆ needles
- ◆ soil
- ◆ pebbles, gravel
- ◆ seeds (marigolds grow quickly)
- ◆ pan

Directions:

1. Punch a hole in the bottom of a plastic cup with a needle.

2. Fill 3/4 of the cup with soil. Mix in pebbles and gravel to help drain the water.

3. Make shallow indentations in the soil with fingers, lay seeds in the holes, and cover with more soil.

4. Predict what will happen to the seeds in the following conditions: light and water, water and no light, light and no water, no light and no water. Write predictions on experience chart paper.

5. Place two cups in the light and two cups in a dark closet. Water one cup in the light and one cup in the dark every other day.

6. After three days, check the seeds for growth. Discuss any changes that have occurred.

7. Check the plants' progress every day or two. When three weeks have passed, place all the cups next to one another. Compare and contrast what happened to the soil and seeds in each cup. Then review the prediction chart to see which predictions came true and which did not.

Spring Bookmarks

Materials:
- glue
- oaktag
- crayons or markers
- scissors
- hole puncher
- yarn

Directions:
1. Reproduce the bookmarks on page 27 once for each child.
2. Help each child mount the bookmarks on oaktag. Then color the bookmarks and cut them out.
3. Punch a hole at the top of each bookmark.
4. Have children thread short lengths of yarn through the holes.

The Selfish Giant Flannel Board

A long time ago, in a very small town, there lived a group of children who played together every day. These children loved to play in a giant's garden, which had beautiful, soft grass and tall, colorful flowers as far as the eye could see.

"We are so very happy here!" the children would say to each other.

Now, the giant himself had been away from his home for seven years. When he returned and saw the children playing in his garden, he became very angry.

"Out of my garden!" he bellowed, and the children ran away as quickly as they could.

"This is my garden, and mine alone," said the giant. "No one may come into my garden but me."

So the selfish giant built a high wall around the garden, and no one dared enter.

The children tried to play in other places around town, but no spot was as nice as the giant's garden.

"We were so very happy there!" they told each other sadly.

When spring arrived, gardens all over town bloomed. The water in the brook gurgled merrily, and the sky was a brilliant blue. But in the selfish giant's garden, spring would not come. The flowers did not want to peek out from under the ground because there were no children around to appreciate their loveliness. The buds on the trees did not turn into leaves because there were no singing birds around to make nests in their branches.

Winter was quite happy, for it could stay in the giant's garden all year long. Snow and frost and ice covered the ground under a blanket of coldness. Fierce winds shook the walls of the giant's castle, which puzzled the selfish giant.

"Why is spring so late this year?" he wondered. "When will winter go away?"

But winter stayed all through summer and autumn. And when the winter season arrived again for the rest of the world, the giant's garden became even more bitter and cold.

The selfish giant felt sadder and sadder. He was tired of winter. He missed his old garden, with the beautiful, soft grass and the tall, colorful flowers.

Then one day the giant heard a beautiful sound coming from outside his window. He looked out to see a little boy and girl singing at the bottom of a tree. The two children had sneaked through a small hole in the garden wall. Miraculously, the blossoms on the trees began to bloom, and birds flying overhead joined the children in song.

The giant felt a warmness surround his heart. And he understood why spring had not come to his garden for so long.

"I have been a most selfish giant," he said. "Now I know that a garden cannot grow without love and sharing."

The giant went right out and knocked down the wall. When the children saw that the giant was no longer mean and uncaring, they all returned to the garden, and together they played with the unselfish giant forever and ever.

The Selfish Giant Flannel Board

Reproduce each of the figures below and on page 31. Color the figures and cut them out. Glue flannel to the backs of the figures and let children move them around a flannel board as they hear the story.

Spring Doorknob Decorations

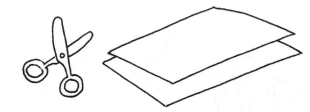

Materials:
- glue
- oaktag
- scissors
- crayons/markers

Directions:
1. Reproduce the doorknob decorations on pages 33-34 once for each child.
2. Have children glue the decorations onto oaktag and cut them out.
3. Let children color and decorate their work.
4. Cut a slit on the right or left side of the doorknob holder, then cut out the center circle, as shown.
5. Children may take home their doorknob decorations to use in their bedrooms or playrooms.

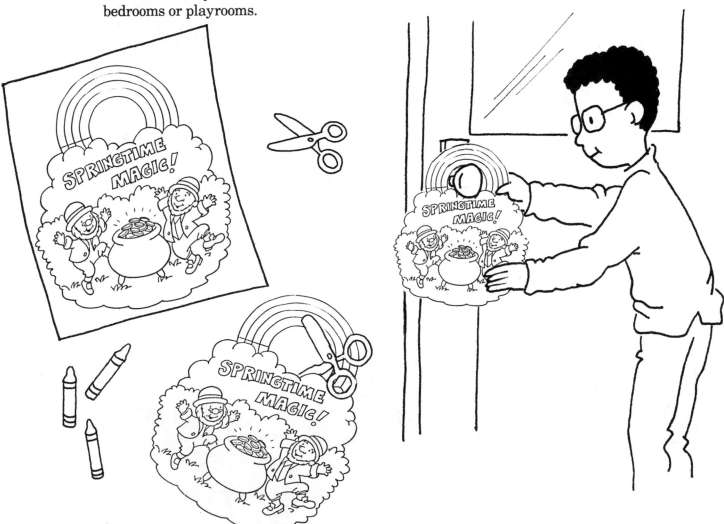

SPRING RIGHT IN!

Name _____

Springtime Animals

Draw a line to match the baby animal
to its parent.

Name _____

From Caterpillar to Butterfly

Cut out the boxes below along the dotted lines. Color the pictures. Then place them in order to show how a caterpillar becomes a butterfly.

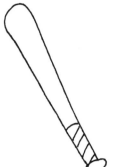

Spring Training Bulletin Board

Shape up your students by using this bulletin board as a spring incentive.

Directions:

1. Draw a large baseball diamond on a bulletin board. Draw each base, the pitcher's mound, and home plate.

2. Reproduce one of the boy or girl runners on pages 38-39 for each child in the class. Give each child a figure and ask him or her to color it, and to write his or her name across the front.

3. Line the baseball player figures up across the bottom of the bulletin board. As soon as a child does something positive (such as accomplishing an assignment or helping out a friend), move that child's "runner" to first base.

4. Each positive task will move the child up another base until he or she "scores" a run. Record each student's scores. After a child has scored a certain number of runs, reward him or her with a special treat.

Name _____

Baseball Action

Across
1. The shape of the playing field
3. When bat meets ball
5. A player moving from first to second
8. A sharp hit
9. What a player is in when he isn't hitting well

Down
2. The player at the plate facing the pitcher
4. You're not really a thief if you do this to a base
6. The best hit of all
7. A tricky pitch

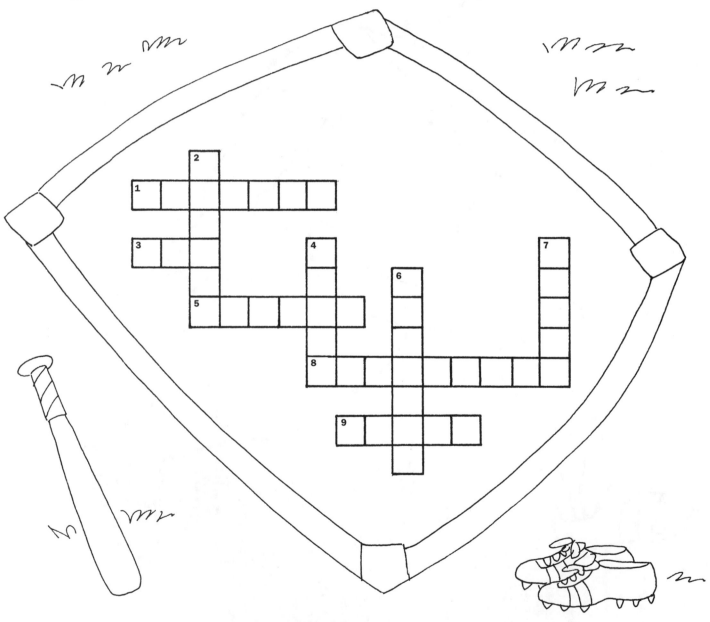

Paint Experiments

Celebrate the birthday of artist Vincent van Gogh, who was born on March 30, 1853, in the Netherlands. Van Gogh was a prolific painter, but sold just one of his paintings in his lifetime. Today his paintings often sell for well over a million dollars.

1. Lay out cups filled with blue, red, and yellow paint. Distribute paper and let children explore what happens when colors are brushed, dabbed, or finger painted on paper, and when colors are mixed. Discuss any new colors formed when two or more colors are combined. Compare and contrast the processes of brushing, dabbing, and finger painting.

2. Allow time for water-color painting as well and compare the techniques used for each medium.

3. Fill a tub or water table with water. Students may pick a color of food coloring and squeeze a few drops into the tub. Watch the color as it mixes with the water and follows any movement in the water. Predict what will happen when two colors are mixed in the water. Squeeze in a few drops of different colors, one at a time.

4. Give students prisms and glasses with colored lenses with which to experiment. Encourage them to describe what they see when looking through these objects.

Finger Paint Fun

Materials:
- ◆ 1 cup cold water
- ◆ 1/2 cup cornstarch
- ◆ 3 cups boiling water
- ◆ food coloring or tempera paints
- ◆ 1/2 teaspoon salt
- ◆ finger paint paper
- ◆ newspaper
- ◆ damp sponge

Directions:
1. Mix the water and cornstarch until the cornstarch dissolves.
2. Pour the mixture into the boiling water, add salt, and stir until shiny.
3. Cool the mixture. Add food coloring for color.
4. Because this activity can be very messy, it should be done with just a few children at a time. Place newspaper on the floor around a table. Use a damp sponge and wipe the table to make it moist.
5. Spoon a few blobs of the paint onto the table. (Make sure the artists are well covered!) Students may paint right on the table.
6. When they have a design they wish to keep, have the children stand away from the table. Lay a piece of paper over the design and press down gently. Starting at one corner, slowly raise the paper and lay to dry on a flat surface.

The Right to Vote

Explain to the class that the Fifteenth Amendment to the Constitution was added on March 30, 1870. It prohibits states from denying the right of anyone to vote based on race, color, or previous condition of servitude.

1. Hold an election with the class. Tell them that they will be voting on what to do during their free time that day: reading or extra outdoor time. Exclude members of the class wearing blue (or some other color) from the vote. Tell them that they absolutely have no say in the vote.

2. Ask students how they felt about this election. Did they feel it was a fair and accurate representation of the class's wishes? How did excluded students feel when they were told they were not allowed to vote? How did students who were allowed to vote feel?

3. Elicit what might happen when a group of people with specific needs or wants has no opportunity to make their voices heard. Inform students that the vote was an activity designed to show how people feel and act when they identify something as unfair.

4. Distribute large pieces of paper for students to create posters showing support for the Fifteenth Amendment. Ask them to pretend they are living in the 1860s and want to get the amendment passed. They may draw pictures or make up slogans for their posters.

Women We Admire

Although men from all races and colors could vote in 1870, women were excluded from all elections held in the United States until the Nineteenth Amendment went into effect on August 26, 1920. One of the leaders of the women's suffrage movement was Susan B. Anthony, who worked most of her adult life trying to win the right to vote for women.

In honor of Women's History Month in March, ask students to interview a woman they admire most. The person may be a relative, a neighbor, a teacher, or their doctor. Students should ask about the subject's childhood, when she made a decision about the direction of her life, what her day is like, what her hopes and dreams are, what she likes to do, and any other relevant questions. When the interviews are completed, ask students to share them with the class and encourage the children to ask questions or make comments.

Invite women into the classroom to discuss their jobs, special talents, and interests. Try to invite women with jobs that are usually gender-stereotyped by children, such as firefighters, sanitation workers, doctors, or police officers. Women senior citizens would also be a valuable addition to this topic. They could share how women were treated and what careers women were limited to when they were young as opposed to the opportunities offered to women today.

Women's History Month Class Book

Take students to the school or local library to borrow books about women they admire. Children may write about the selected women and what they did to help change the image of women.

Encourage children to imagine what the world might be like without women doctors, police officers, politicians, astronauts, actresses and singers, artists, and activists. Who would speak up for other women who are not famous? Who would be the role models for little girls trying to decide what to be when they grow up? If women of long ago had not stood up and made themselves known, would women today have the same job opportunities, the right to vote, and confidence in themselves? Share reports and thoughts on the subject with the class.

Egg Candles

Materials:

- ◆ water
- ◆ small saucepan
- ◆ paraffin, crayons, candles
- ◆ tin can
- ◆ hot plate
- ◆ eggshells
- ◆ craft sticks
- ◆ thick string
- ◆ egg cartons
- ◆ spoons or small measuring cup
- ◆ paints and paintbrushes
- ◆ markers

Directions:

1. Pour water into a small saucepan and place it on a hot plate. Place paraffin, crayons, and candles of the desired color into a tin can. Then place the tin can into the pan of water.

2. While the paraffin is melting, prepare the eggshells. Discard the tops, leaving 3/4 intact. Place the eggshells in the egg carton to help keep them upright.

3. Tie a piece of string onto the middle of a craft stick. Lay the stick across the opening of the eggshell. Make sure the string touches the bottom of the shell.

4. When the paraffin has melted, pour it into the eggshell with a spoon or small measuring cup until the wax is about 1" from the top. Caution children that the wax, hot plate, and tin can will be very hot.

5. When the wax has hardened, children may wish to decorate their eggshells with markers or paint.

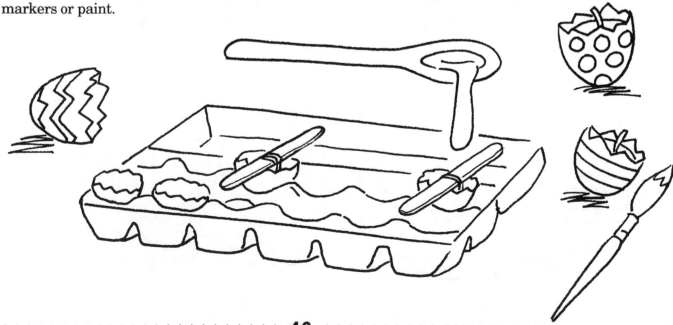

Easter Egg "War"

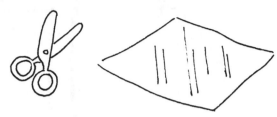

Materials:
◆ crayons or markers
◆ scissors
◆ clear contact paper

Directions:
1. Reproduce the egg patterns on page 48 nine times. Color the eggs and cut them out.

2. On the plain side, write a number from 1 to 10. Cover with clear contact paper.

3. Two to four children may play this card game. Each player places a card number side up. The player with the largest number takes all the cards that have just been played. If players have the same number showing, they must go to "war."

4. The players with the same value of cards then place three cards with the number facedown. The fourth card is turned faceup. Whoever has the largest number showing wins all the cards in that hand. If those fourth cards also show the same number, the third card is flipped over and the one with the larger number wins the hand.

5. Play continues until one player has all the cards.

Easter Egg Sort

Materials:

- ◆ crayons or markers
- ◆ scissors

Directions:

1. Reproduce the egg patterns from page 48 five times. Cut out the eggs and give one to each child. Ask students to color the eggs.

2. Divide the class into small groups and have them compare and contrast their eggs (i.e., patterns, designs, colors).

3. Sort the eggs into categories within each group according to some attribute(s).

4. Invite the other groups over to one group to see how they have sorted their eggs. Ask students to guess why they grouped the eggs the way they did. If no one can guess, the featured group may explain. Rotate the groups so each one gets a turn to explain how they categorized their eggs.

The Story of Passover

Ask students if anyone if familiar with the story of Passover. Explain to the children that Passover is the Jewish festival that celebrates the deliverance of the Israelites from slavery in Egypt many years ago. Tell students that Passover occurs in the months of March or April, and lasts for eight days.

Jewish people celebrate the first two nights of Passover with a feast called a seder. Families and friends gather together to retell the Passover story. Each person at the gathering reads from the Haggadah, a book that tells the story of Passover.

Special foods are served at seders. Matzoh, a kind of unleavened bread the Israelites took with them as they fled from Egypt, is the only bread eaten during Passover. Other Passover foods include hard-boiled eggs, parsley, bitter herbs, and a mixture of apples, almonds, cinnamon, and wine. Each of these foods symbolizes part of the Passover story.

Have a classroom seder to celebrate Passover. Serve matzoh and other traditional foods. Explain the difference between unleavened bread and other breads.

Favorite Foods Place Mat

Celebrate National Nutrition Month in March by making this place mat with your class.

Materials:
- ◆ crayons and markers
- ◆ scissors
- ◆ 12" x 18" construction paper
- ◆ old workbooks and magazines
- ◆ glue
- ◆ clear contact paper

Directions:

1. Distribute crayons or markers, scissors, and construction paper to students. Ask the children to draw pictures of their favorite foods, or cut out pictures from old workbooks and magazines.

2. When enough pictures have been collected by each child to cover most of a 12" x 18" piece of construction paper, have each student glue the pictures onto the paper in a collage.

3. After the glue has dried, cover the collage with clear contact paper.

4. Write the names of the four food groups on a chalkboard. Then ask volunteers to name some of the foods on their place mats and identify the groups to which these foods belong.

5. Students may use their place mats at home, or in school for lunch or snack time.

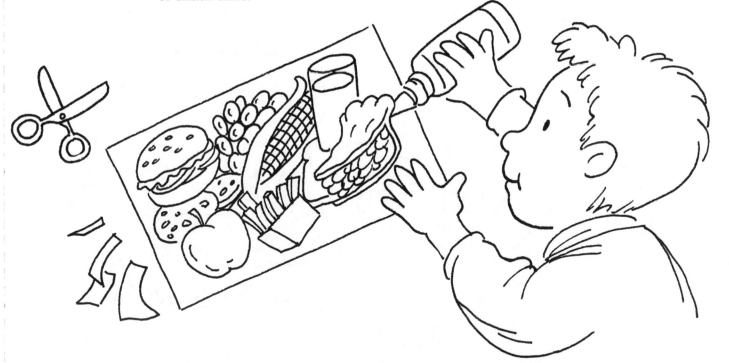

An Alphabet of Food Book

Materials:
- ◆ 9" x 12" construction paper
- ◆ crayons or markers
- ◆ scissors
- ◆ old workbooks and magazines
- ◆ glue
- ◆ hole puncher
- ◆ yarn

Directions:

1. Distribute a 9" x 12" piece of construction paper to each child. Ask each student to draw the letter A, upper- and lowercase, on the paper with crayon or marker. Be sure to tell students to use the entire page when drawing their letters.

2. Have the children draw pictures of foods that begin with the letter A within the letter's lines, or cut out pictures from old workbooks and magazines and glue them within the lines.

3. Over the course of several weeks, ask students to repeat this exercise for each letter of the alphabet.

4. If the children cannot draw or find pictures for some letters, encourage them to create a new kind of food for those letters.

5. When each of the letters of the alphabet has been represented on a page, have students gather the pages together in order. Encourage the children to make covers for their Alphabet Food Books.

6. Punch three holes in the left sides of the papers and bind together with yarn.

Fooled You!

Explain to the children how April Fool's Day came to be. Tell them that long ago, some countries celebrated the new year on April 1. When the calendar was changed and the new year began on January 1, some people did not know. These people, who would celebrate the new year on the old date, were known as April Fools. Today we celebrate this day by playing funny tricks on people and trying to **make them** look foolish.

Help the children make April Fool's Day masks by following the directions below.

Materials:
- ◆ crayons or markers
- ◆ scissors
- ◆ oaktag
- ◆ clear contact paper
- ◆ clear tape

Directions:
1. Reproduce the glasses, eyebrows, and nose patterns on page 54 once for each child. Have students color the patterns and mount them on oaktag.
2. Tell the children to cut out the patterns, then cover them with clear contact paper.
3. Show students how to bend the glasses at the sides and the big nose down the middle. Attach the nose to the bridge of the glasses and the eyebrows above the glasses with clear tape.
4. Wrap the stems of the glasses around the backs of ears and center the nose, as shown. Tell the children to see how many people they can fool with their disguises!

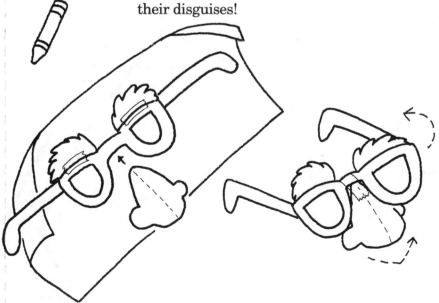

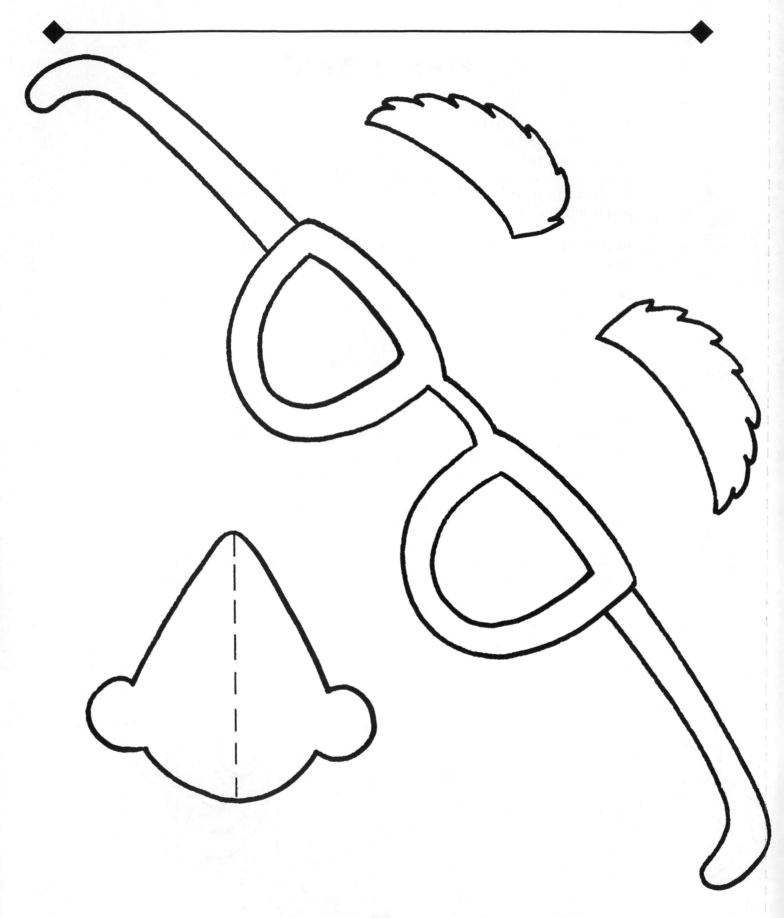

Name _____

You Can't Fool Me!

Circle the clown on the right that is identical to the one on the left.

Guess-and-Peek Folders

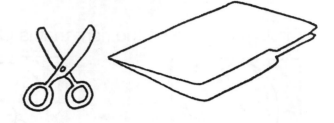

Materials:

◆ scissors
◆ old workbooks and magazines
◆ glue
◆ file folders

Directions:

1. Cut out large pictures of animals, people, and objects from old workbooks and magazines.

2. Glue each picture to the inside of a file folder.

3. Cut a small square from the front cover of the folder to reveal a tiny portion of the picture inside the folder, as shown.

4. Write a question about the picture on the front cover, such as "Who has ears like these?" or "What has wheels like these?"

5. Show students the folders, one at a time, and ask them the questions. Encourage them to look closely at the portion revealed in the square and make a guess.

6. Leave the folders out on a bookshelf so students may look at them during free time.

Class Census

April 1 is Census Day. Tell students that a census is a type of poll that is taken every ten years to find out important information about a country. Census takers try to count how many people live in each town, city, county, state, and the whole country. This information is used to help figure out government representation, how tax dollars are spent, and many other things.

Ask the children to come up with questions to take a class census. Some suggestions are family size, ages of students, likes and dislikes, and career aspirations. Write the questions down on a large piece of oaktag.

Create a graph on the chalkboard to mark the results of the census poll. Ask students to raise their hands in response to each question. When all the results have been recorded, help the class make inferences from the information. Show how the class census can help determine what material is covered in class. For example, if a majority of the students say that their favorite subject is reading, you may wish to assign special work in this area.

BROTHERS	SISTERS	DOGS	CATS
|||	ⱶⱵⱵ ||	||||	ⱶⱵⱵ |||

Once Upon a Time...

Hans Christian Andersen was born on April 2, 1805 in Odense, Denmark. His family was very poor, and his father died when Hans was only 11 years old. With the help of a friend, Hans was able to get a royal scholarship and receive an education. He later became a writer, and was best known for his fairy tales for children. Some of his stories are "The Little Mermaid," "The Fir Tree," "The Ugly Duckling," "Little Claus and Big Claus," and "The Emperor's New Clothes."

Ask students to think about what makes a good fairy tale. Encourage them to consider plot, setting, and character development. After discussing the elements of a story, have each student create a fairy tale of his or her own. Point out to the children that fairy tales often have moral endings, which point out the virtues of good behavior and the consequences of bad behavior.

Have students draw pictures to accompany their stories. When all the stories are completed, place them in the reading center for everyone to see.

The Princess and the Pea Flannel Board

Once upon a time there was a prince who wanted to marry a real princess. The prince traveled far and wide looking for the right young woman. Many fair maidens told the prince that they were princesses, but he could never be sure that they were true princesses. After several years of searching, the prince sadly returned to his castle, certain that he would never find a bride.

Then, one dark, stormy night, someone knocked on the castle door. The prince answered the door, and there before him stood a beautiful princess. The princess was soaked to the bone and stood shivering in the cold wind.

"May I come in?" she asked pitifully.

The prince opened the door and let her in.

"Who are you?" he asked curiously.

"I am a princess," she said.

"Are you a real princess?" asked the prince.

"Of course," said the princess.

But the prince couldn't be certain. He decided to think of a way to discover if the young woman was a true princess.

The prince went to the bedroom where the princess was to spend the night. He stacked mattress after mattress on top of each other, until the pile nearly reached the ceiling. Then he placed a single tiny pea under the bottom mattress.

"There!" he said, quite pleased with himself. "Now we will see if she is really a princess."

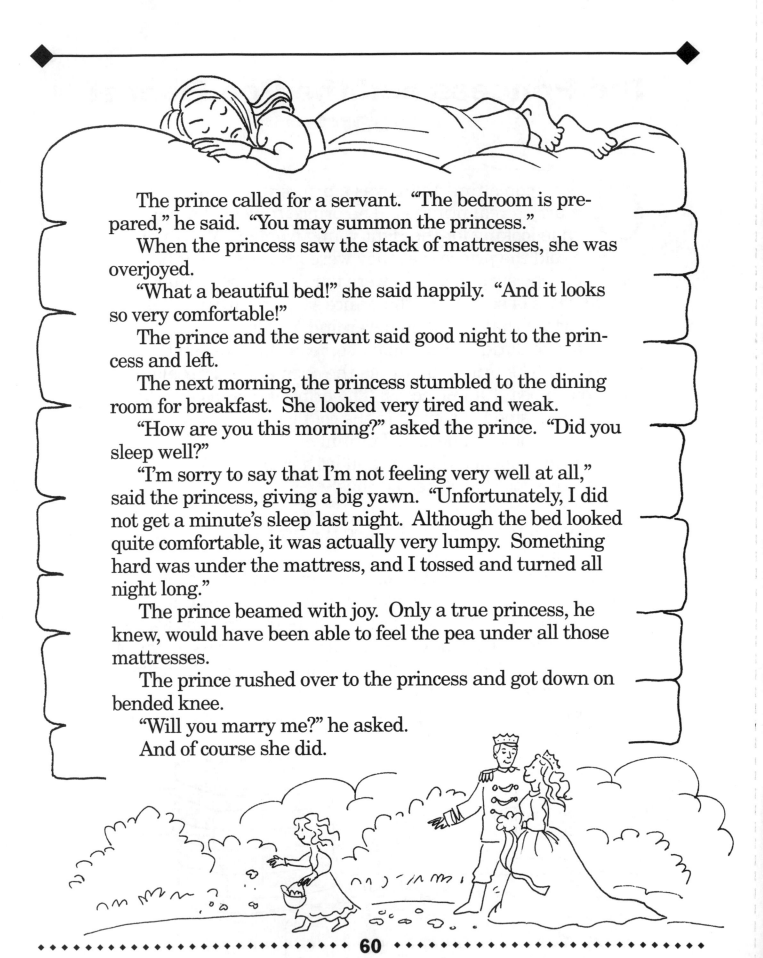

The prince called for a servant. "The bedroom is prepared," he said. "You may summon the princess."

When the princess saw the stack of mattresses, she was overjoyed.

"What a beautiful bed!" she said happily. "And it looks so very comfortable!"

The prince and the servant said good night to the princess and left.

The next morning, the princess stumbled to the dining room for breakfast. She looked very tired and weak.

"How are you this morning?" asked the prince. "Did you sleep well?"

"I'm sorry to say that I'm not feeling very well at all," said the princess, giving a big yawn. "Unfortunately, I did not get a minute's sleep last night. Although the bed looked quite comfortable, it was actually very lumpy. Something hard was under the mattress, and I tossed and turned all night long."

The prince beamed with joy. Only a true princess, he knew, would have been able to feel the pea under all those mattresses.

The prince rushed over to the princess and got down on bended knee.

"Will you marry me?" he asked.

And of course she did.

Reproduce each of the figures below and on page 62. Color the figures and cut them out. Glue flannel to the backs of the figures and let children move them around a flannel board as they hear the story.

Our Favorite Books

To celebrate International Children's Book Day on April 2, ask students to name their favorite books, authors, and illustrators. Write these favorites on the chalkboard.

Ask the children to talk about why they like a particular author, illustrator, or book. Then have students find the books they like in the school library, or in their own libraries. Tell each child to write a paragraph describing why he or she likes the particular book, and accompany the paragraph with an illustration of a scene from the book.

Afterwards, have the children write to authors or illustrators, asking them questions about the books. When students receive responses to their letters, encourage them to share the authors' comments with the rest of the class.

The Pony Express

Ask the children if anyone knows what the Pony Express was. This method of distributing mail during America's frontier expansion was founded on April 3, 1860. Riders traveled in relays between St. Joseph, Missouri, and Sacramento, California. The "stations" on the Pony Express were located every 10-15 miles across the country. Each rider carried the mail in a leather saddle bag, and received a fresh pony or horse at each station. This relay method cut down the amount of time it took to deliver a letter to the west from three weeks or more to only ten days.

The Pony Express riders traveled in all types of weather, and often risked their lives to see that the mail was delivered as quickly as possible. However, it was a short-lived operation. After the transcontinental telegraph was put into use in 1861, there was no longer a need for the Pony Express.

Help the children research this time period of western expansion. Then ask students to pretend that they are traveling out west, or have settled in a new area on the frontier. Provide students with story starters to write their own letters "home," telling what sights they have seen and what changes they have experienced in their lives. Some suggestions are:

> *I am writing to you by our campfire. We are about to head up into the mountains. I hope...*

> *We have finally settled in California. The land here is so beautiful. I can't wait to...*

> *The last week of our journey has been difficult. After we crossed a raging river, we came across...*

> *Pa has finished building our sod house on the prairie. I helped him with it. We met some of our neighbors. They are...*

> *I know we have only just begun our journey to California, but some exciting things have already happened. First,...*

Excellence in Education Award Ceremony

Booker T. Washington was born into slavery on April 5, 1856. After he became free, he went on to become a great educator and advisor to presidents. Booker T. Washington founded the Tuskegee Institute in 1881. He believed the way to succeed was through education.

Hold an education awards ceremony with the class. Reproduce the pattern on page 66 once for each child. Write each child's name on a certificate and the area in which he or she succeeds. Invite students' parents to the ceremony. Call each child in turn to the front of the room to accept his or her award. Make sure there is one for each student. Roll the award and tie it with ribbon to add an extra touch to the ceremony. Ask any participants if they wish to say a few words about education and school. If desired, serve refreshments after the ceremony so classroom parents can meet one another.

This Excellence in Education Award

is for

in the area of

Excellence in Education.

Teacher

Date

Sports Day

Inform the class that the first modern Olympic Games were held in Greece on April 6, 1896. Then tell students that they will stage their own "Olympic Games" by having a spring Sports Day.

Ask the children to suggest some events for Sports Day. Events may be for individuals or teams. Some suggestions are:

- ◆ leapfrog relay
- ◆ three-legged race
- ◆ chin-ups
- ◆ sack races
- ◆ broad jump
- ◆ obstacle course race
- ◆ kickball
- ◆ rope climb
- ◆ tumbling
- ◆ basketball shooting

Let the class set up the distances and requirements for each event. In the week before the Sports Day celebration, give students time to practice for the events they are entering.

Invite parents, friends, school workers, and other classes to participate or watch the Sports Day events. Encourage everyone to bring a sack lunch and beverage to enjoy during the games.

To make awards for Sports Day, reproduce the ribbons on page 68. Mount each ribbon on oaktag. Color the ribbons and cut them out. Write each child's name and event on the ribbon as appropriate.

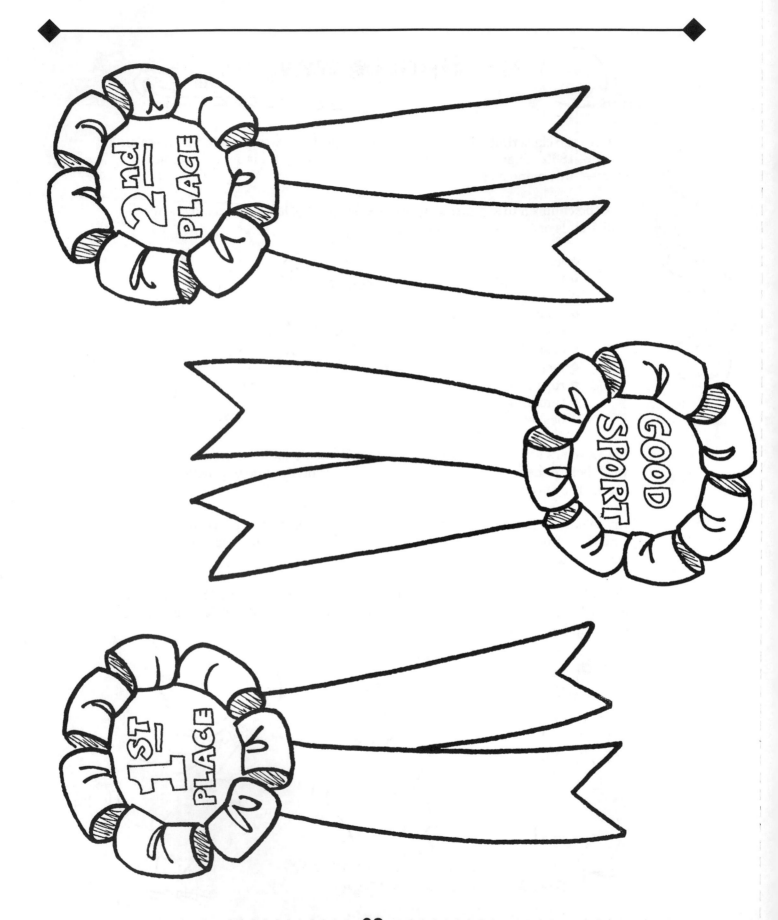

Name _____

North Pole Search

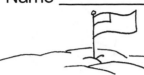

Admiral Robert E. Peary was an American explorer who discovered the North Pole on April 6, 1909. He first tried to reach the North Pole in 1898-1902, then tried again in 1905-06. He finally reached his goal with his assistant and four Inuits at his side. At the North Pole, Peary and his crew performed experiments that showed that the sea around the North Pole was much deeper than people had previously believed.

Find the 10 hidden words in the puzzle below. Words can run across, down, crosswise, and backwards.

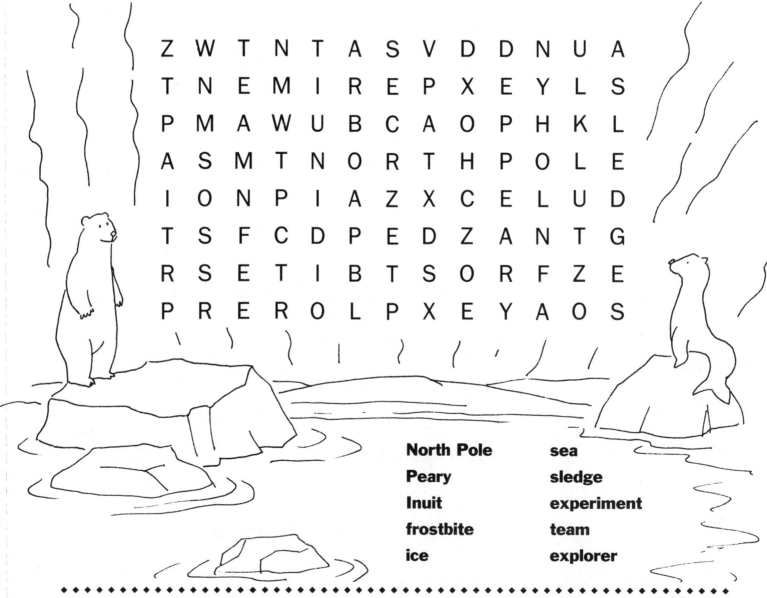

```
Z W T N T A S V D D N U A
T N E M I R E P X E Y L S
P M A W U B C A O P H K L
A S M T N O R T H P O L E
I O N P I A Z X C E L U D
T S F C D P E D Z A N T G
R S E T I B T S O R F Z E
P R E R O L P X E Y A O S
```

North Pole   **sea**

Peary   **sledge**

Inuit   **experiment**

frostbite   **team**

ice   **explorer**

Name _____

Outer Space Voyage

On April 12, 1961, Yuri A. Gagarin, from the former U.S.S.R., became the first astronaut to orbit the earth in a spaceship. Other manned space flights soon followed. The first astronaut to walk on the moon was Neil Armstrong, from the American Apollo XI flight, on July 20, 1969.

Look up the following words in a dictionary. Then draw lines to match each word to its definition.

spacecraft   prefix meaning star

accelerate   the path of an object in space as it revolves around another body

aerospace   the part of a space flight when a spacecraft starts to come down through the atmosphere

astro-   a manmade object that travels through space

gravity   the Earth's atmosphere and the areas of space beyond it

reentry   to increase speed

astronaut   pulls things on Earth

orbit   a person who travels in space

Name _____

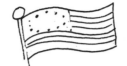

Paul Revere's Ride

Fill in the blanks for each sentence, using the boxed words at the bottom of the page.

1. Paul Revere rode from _____ to

_____ , Massachusetts on April 18, 1775.

2. He fought on the side of the _____ during

the _____ War.

3. Paul Revere warned the American patriots that

the_____ were coming.

4. His bravery inspired a poem by _____

called "Paul Revere's Ride."

5. Paul Revere also participated in the _____

on December 16, 1773.

6. After the Revolutionary War was won by the patriots, Paul

Revere returned to his job as a _____ .

British	**patriots**
silversmith	**Lexington**
Boston	**Boston Tea Party**
Revolutionary	**Henry Wadsworth Longfellow**

Class Science Fair

Hold a class science fair in honor of Earth Day on April 22. Inform students in the class that they will be hosting the science fair about three months before the scheduled event. Explain that they may invent a machine or other object, or design an experiment which proves or disproves a theory. Their entries may also revolve around the importance of saving our environment and other ecological exhibits.

Think up various science stations to show what students have been working on during the year (i.e., animals, plants, magnets, food). Ask students to create posters to be displayed in the school giving the date, time, place, and types of entries wanted. Don't forget to send a letter home informing parents of this special event.

The day before students are to bring in their projects, set up display stations around the classroom. Arrange any science posters you may have around the room. Make sure stations are located so people will have easy access to them, and the flow around them will not be obstructed.

Ask older children to write an article reviewing the science fair, including very brief interviews with participants and observers on their thoughts about the event.

Name _____

  Recycling Checklist

Which of these items do your recycle in your house?

aluminum cans

colored glass

clear glass

plastic

newspapers

glossy paper

batteries

toxic materials (paint, etc.)

Name some other ways that you recycle.

_____

_____

_____

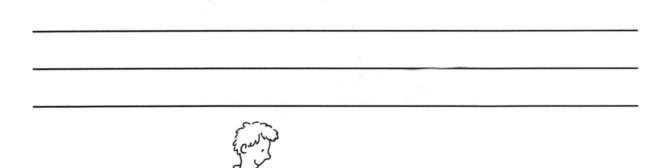

Pollution Solutions

Ask students the following questions about garbage:

◆ Where does your garbage go?
◆ If it goes to a dump, what should we do with the garbage when the dump is full?
◆ If it goes to an incinerator, what should we do to decrease the pollution coming from the burning garbage?
◆ If it is dumped in the ocean, what will happen to ocean life when there is too much garbage?

Give students time to think up suggestions for garbage disposal. Then help the class compose letters to a local assemblyperson and to the sanitation department asking for information about garbage disposal in your area. Include the children's suggestions for a healthier disposal system.

Take a survey to see how many students recycle their garbage at home. Ask students to describe the different ways they recycle garbage and conserve energy. If possible, plan a class trip to a recycling plant to find out what happens to the glass, metal, plastic, and paper that is sorted for recycling.

Class Pet Show

Tell children that the first week of May is National Pet Week. Ask volunteers to talk about what pets they have (or what pets they wish they had), and why they like these types of pets.

Elicit from the children what responsibilites are involved in caring for a pet. Do some types of pets require more care and attention than other pets? What type of training is needed for each pet? What types of pets can live outdoors? Why do some animals make better pets than other animals? Write down students' comments on a large piece of oaktag.

Set up a day to have a class pet show. Let students bring in their pets from home to show to their classmates. (Be sure to stress that the pets brought in to school should be comfortable with strangers and new situations so they are not a danger to people or to themselves.) Encourage the children to show off any special tricks or talents their pets have.

After the pet show, ask students to write about their favorite pets and draw pictures to go with their stories. Staple all the stories and illustrations together to make a class book. Title the book "Our Favorite Pets," and place it in the reading center for all to enjoy.

May Day Flowers

Explain to students that long ago, Romans used to have a festival in the spring to celebrate their goddess of flowers, Flora. They would decorate her temple with flowers from the woods and fields. In Great Britain, people continue the tradition of "bringing home the May." They collect flowers and decorate their homes with them. People also give the flowers to friends and neighbors to wish them happiness.

May Day celebrations take place every May 1. Baskets of flowers are exchanged among friends, traditional folksongs are sung, and people play hoop-rolling games and dance around Maypoles.

Use the flower patterns on pages 77-78 to decorate two Maypoles for the class. (A volleyball net pole works well as a Maypole.) Tape the colored flowers and streamers onto the net poles until they are covered. At the top of each pole, securely attach 12 braided (for added strength) streamers which will reach about 10' out from the pole.

Choose 12 children to hold the ends of the 12 streamers on each pole. Place the children in a circle around their Maypoles, with six students facing clockwise, and six facing counterclockwise. (Each pair will be back to back.) Instruct the children that when the music begins, they are to weave in and out of each other while staying in the circle. Encourage students to whisper to themselves while they move, "In...out...in...out," so they remember the sequence. Allow students to have a practice run without the streamers if necessary. The group that weaves their streamers down to the bottom first is the winner.

Piñata Party!

Materials:

- ◆ crayons or markers
- ◆ scissors
- ◆ oaktag
- ◆ glue
- ◆ collage materials
- ◆ tissue paper
- ◆ bags of treats
- ◆ masking tape
- ◆ hole punch
- ◆ thick string or yarn
- ◆ plastic bat or wooden yardstick

Directions:

1. Reproduce the piñata patterns on pages 80-81. Color the patterns and cut them out.

2. Glue the bull head and legs in place on the body. Decorate with collage materials and tissue paper if desired.

3. Trace the bull onto oaktag two times. Then glue the bull onto one oaktag outline.

4. Squeeze a line of glue around the inside edges of the oaktag bull outline, leaving a 6" gap in its back. Lay the decorated bull on top and press together gently, as shown.

5. Fill the piñata with one treat bag for each child. Reinforce the opening of the piñata with masking tape, then punch four holes about 1" in along the edges. Thread the holes with string or yarn long enough to reach up to the ceiling. Punch two holes in the top of the piñata, then hang it from the ceiling and knot securely.

6. Ask the children to come forward one at a time with a plastic bat or wooden yardstick to hit the piñata and try to break it open.

When the piñata opens and the treat bags fall, each child may scramble forward and get a bag.

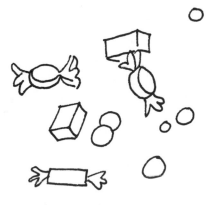

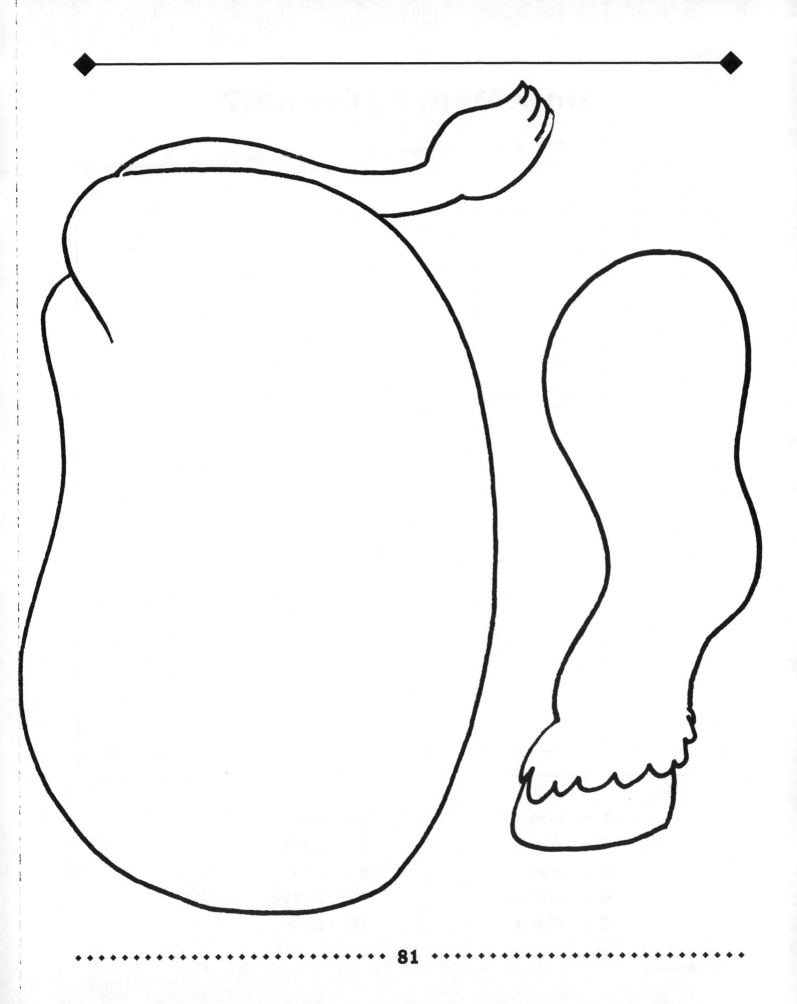

Name _____

How Many? ¿Cuánto?

Count the objects in each group. Then write the Spanish word for that number on the line provided.

_____   _____   _____   _____   _____

_____   _____   _____   _____   _____

1 =	uno	6 =	seis
2 =	dos	7 =	siete
3 =	tres	8 =	ocho
4 =	cuatro	9 =	nueve
5 =	cinco	10 =	diez

Teacher Recognition Day

Help students organize a Teacher Recognition Day celebration for May 8. Begin by discussing the responsibilities of a teacher. Ask the children what type of training a person needs before he or she can teach. Elicit comments from students about what qualities a good teacher possesses. Write the comments on a large piece of oaktag.

After the discussion, tell the class that each child may be the "teacher" for part of the day. Divide the day into sections to ensure that all the major subject areas will be covered. Tell the children that they must be well organized and prepare their "lessons" ahead of time. Guide students with their lesson plans and help them think of interesting projects and activities. Tell the children to refer to the comments written on the oaktag chart.

After Teacher Recognition Day, ask students to use their experiences to write about teaching. Some topics may include:

◆ If I Were a Teacher
◆ What It Takes to Be a Good Teacher
◆ Why I Want to Be a Teacher
◆ My Favorite Teacher

Attach the essays to a classroom wall or a bulletin board under the heading "Today's Teachers."

Mother's Day Gifts

Refrigerator Magnet

Materials:

- ◆ crayons or markers
- ◆ white paper
- ◆ glue
- ◆ oaktag
- ◆ scissors
- ◆ clear polyurethane
- ◆ paintbrush
- ◆ magnets
- ◆ tissue paper
- ◆ ribbons

Directions:

1. Ask each child to create a small picture (about 2" high) on white paper to use to make a magnet.
2. Have students mount their pictures on oaktag and cut them out.
3. Coat each picture with clear polyurethane.
4. Tell students to glue magnets to the backs of their pictures.
5. Wrap the magnets in tissue paper and tie with ribbons to complete the Mother's Day gifts.

Mother's Day Gifts

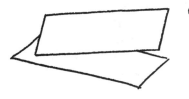

Coupon Book

Materials:
- ◆ 4" x 8" strips of construction paper
- ◆ crayons or markers
- ◆ stapler

Directions:
1. Give each child six 4" x 8" strips of construction paper.
2. Have each student think of five tasks to do for his or her mother. Provide the children with suggestions, such as cleaning the den, doing the dishes, weeding the garden, folding the laundry, taking care of younger siblings, preparing a snack, and so on.
3. After students have decided on the tasks, have them write one task on each coupon. If desired, the children may also illustrate each task.
4. Tell students to make covers for their coupon books. Encourage the children to write "Happy Mother's Day Coupon Book" on the cover of each book.
5. Staple each coupon book together along the left side, as shown.

Mother's Day Card

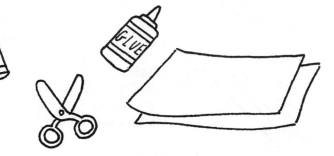

Materials:

- ◆ 12" x 18" construction paper
- ◆ pencil
- ◆ scissors
- ◆ crayons and markers
- ◆ glue

Directions:

1. Give each child a piece of construction paper and demonstrate how to fold it in half widthwise.

2. Have each child mark off two lines, about 2" apart and 2" long, in the middle of the fold. Cut along these lines.

3. Demonstrate how to open the paper, and gently pull the cut section out so that when the paper is folded again the tab will fold into the paper, as shown.

4. Let each child choose one of the Mother's Day patterns on pages 87-88 to use to make a pop-up card. Reproduce the selected pattern once for each child.

5. Have students color the patterns and cut them out. Then show the children how to glue their patterns to the vertical section of the tab so that it appears to be standing out from the background, as shown.

6. Lay the paper flat and draw a background and a foreground for the pattern. When the paper is folded again, gently pull the tab in again.

7. Have each child glue the card to another piece of paper, folded in half the same way.

8. Tell students to write greetings on the fronts and insides of their cards. For example, a child may wish to write "To Mom" on the front of the card, and "I love you a whole bunch! Happy Mother's Day!" on the inside of the card.

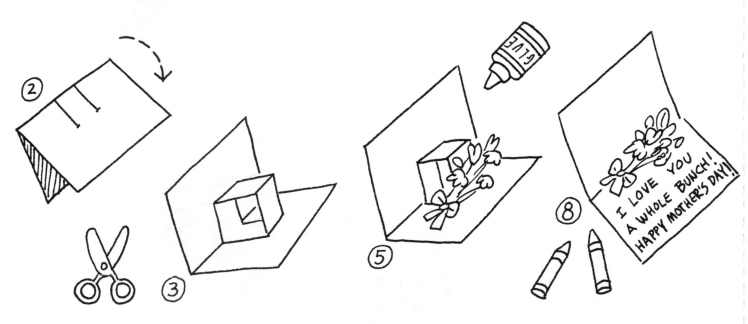

Best Books About Moms

◆ *The Mother's Day Mice*, by Eve Bunting (Ticknor & Fields, 1988)

◆ *Are You My Mother?*, by P.D. Eastman (Random House, 1960)

◆ *I Can Be a Mother*, by Christine Fitz-Gerald (Childrens Press, 1988)

◆ *A Gift for Mama*, by Esther Hautzig (Peter Smith, 1992)

◆ *Happy Mother's Day*, by Steven Kroll (Holiday House, 1985)

◆ *A Birthday Present for Mama*, by Nicole Lorian (Random House, 1984)

◆ *Surprise!*, by Mary Morgan (Viking, 1988)

◆ *Love You Forever*, by Robert Munsch (Firefly Books Ltd., 1986)

◆ *Mother's Day*, by Mary Kay Phelan (HarperCollins, 1965)

◆ *Hooray for Mother's Day!*, by Marjorie Sharmat (Holiday House, 1986)

We Remember

Explain to the class that Memorial Day is a day on which we remember those brave people who died while serving in the Armed Forces. Men and women may serve in a wide variety of areas: army, marines, air force, and navy. The army and marines are usually used on the ground, the air force in the sky, and the navy on the sea, although each of these areas has other specialties as well. We can distinguish military people from civilians by the way they dress: each branch has its own distinct uniforms.

Discuss people the children may know who are part of the military. Encourage children to explain which branch of the armed forces the people joined, the uniform worn, and any other interesting details they may wish to add. Talk about the purpose of the military (protecting the country). Tell students that soldiers may be shipped to different countries to serve, or they may stay in their own country. Some soldiers go to war if that becomes necessary.

Ask volunteers to give a definition of war. Discuss how soldiers might feel knowing they must go and fight. Elicit specific emotions and reasons from children. Ask how they would feel if they had to go to war. The next time children see a parade for those who died while serving in the military, remind them to stop and think about the armed forces.

Our Ancestors

In recognition of Flag Day (June 14), discuss the evolution of the American flag. Explain to the class that the first flag designed by Betsy Ross had 13 stars, which symbolized the original 13 colonies in America. Today's American flag has 50 stars along with 13 stripes that represent the founding colonies.

Ask students to describe the ethnic backgrounds of their own families. How many students were born in a foreign country? Ask each child to discuss his or her family history at home. How many generations have lived in the city, state, or country? What country did his or her family come from originally?

After students have researched their family backgrounds, have them look up information about the countries from which their families came. Ask each child to write a short report about what life was like in this country (or countries) long ago, and what it is like today. Encourage students to draw pictures of the flags that represent these countries, and discover what the components of the flags symbolize.

When all the reports have been completed, ask students to share their research with the rest of the class. If desired, make photocopies of the reports for each child to compile into a class book.

Father's Day Name Plaque

Materials:

- flour
- salt
- lukewarm water
- bowls
- wooden spoons
- rolling pin
- wax paper
- plastic knives
- paintbrushes
- paints
- felt
- glue
- clear polyurethane

Directions:

1. Have each child mix together about 3 cups of flour with 3/4 cup of salt.
2. Tell students to mix well before adding about 1 cup of lukewarm water.
3. Help the children knead the dough until it is mixed smoothly.
4. Roll the dough into a cylinder on wax paper. Then flatten the dough on three sides as shown to make it triangle-shaped.
5. Cut off the edges to make them blunt, as shown.
6. Roll the remaining dough thinly. Have each child make letters from the dough to write "Dad" or his or her father's first name. Put the letters on the triangle-shaped dough plaques.
7. Bake the name plaques at 325° F until they turn golden brown in color.
8. After the plaques have completely cooled, let children paint them. Paint each plaque with a clear coat of polyurethane.
9. Give each child a piece of felt to glue to the bottom of the name plaque.

Father's Day Card

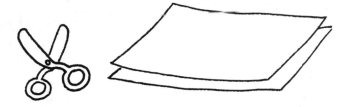

Materials:
- ◆ crayons and markers
- ◆ scissors
- ◆ construction paper
- ◆ glue

Directions:

1. Reproduce the Father's Day card pattern on page 94 once for each child. Have students color the cards and cut them out.

2. Ask each child to fold a 9" x 12" piece of construction paper in half widthwise. Glue the Father's Day card to the front of the paper, as shown.

3. Encourage the children to decorate the fronts and insides of their cards.

4. Have each student write a special Father's Day message inside the card before signing his or her own name.

Best Books About Dads

◆ *Just Like Daddy,* by Frank Asch (Simon & Schuster, 1984)

◆ *I'm Too Small, You're Too Big*, by Judi Barrett (Atheneum, 1981)

◆ *The Little Father*, by Gelett Burgess (Farrar Straus & Giroux, 1987)

◆ *I Can Be a Father*, by Patrick Clinton (Children's Press, 1988)

◆ *Handsomest Father*, by Deborah Hautzig (Greenwillow, 1979)

◆ *Daddy Makes the Best Spaghetti*, by Anna Grossnickel Hines (Clarion, 1988)

◆ *Happy Father's Day*, by Steven Kroll (Holiday House, 1988)

◆ *Hooray for Father's Day!*, by Marjorie Sharmat (Holiday House, 1987)

◆ *Daddy and Ben Together*, by Miriam Stecher (Lothrop Lee, 1981)

◆ *Daddy Is a Monster...Sometimes*, by John Steptoe (HarperCollins, 1980)

Answers

Page 7
Things in the picture that begin with the letter "L" include lamb, lamp, letter, lettuce, lemon, lollipop, lion, and legs.

Answers will vary for Part 2.

Page 35
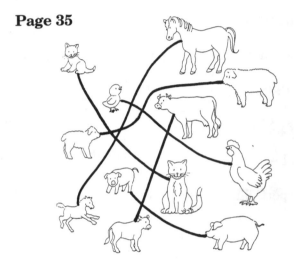

Page 36

Page 40

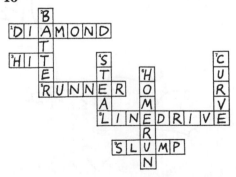

Page 55
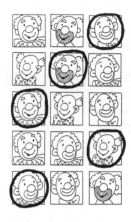

Page 69

```
Z W T N T A S V D D N U A
T N E M I R E P X E Y L S
P M A W U B C A O P H K L
A S M T N O R T H P O L E
I O N P I A Z X C E L U D
T S F C D P E D Z A N T G
R S E T I B T S O R F Z E
P R E R O L P X E Y A O S
```

Page 71
1. Paul Revere rode from Boston to Lexington, Massachusetts on April 18, 1775.
2. He fought on the side of the patriots during the Revolutionary War.
3. Paul Revere warned the American patriots that the British were coming.
4. His bravery inspired a poem by Henry Wadsworth Longfellow called "Paul Revere's Ride."
5. Paul Revere also participated in the Boston Tea Party on December 16, 1773.
6. After the Revolutionary War was won by the patriots, Paul Revere returned to his job as a silversmith.

Page 82
tres, ocho, cinco, siete, cuatro
dos, diez, seis, uno, nueve